COURTSHIP : Every Ways To Keep Your Man

By

D. R Alicia Fung

Table Of Contents

INTRODUCTION

Most young ladies have been drifting in and out of unsuccessful relationship, not realizing it is possible to have more control over future relationships than you have had in the past. It is , possible to learn behaviours that will help move a relationship to forward to commitment. Most singles rush into what they believe is the perfect relationship. When the relationship fails, hurry into the next one. This pattern is likely repeated over and without much thought being given to it. love works the dynamics of sustaining love, or what love is and is not. This book," HOW TO MAKE YOUR MAN COME FOR MORE OF YOU?" will help you to learn how to manage romance for its great result. ! encourage you to read every word of the book, I hope you'll also be challenged in those areas where you've made too many mistakes too often. Love and appreciate him instead of criticising your partner. Even if you most register some negative observation, let it be done in love. lways forgive, put away pride, malice and selfishness from you but let your word be seasoned with “please’ “thank you’ and “sorry

Module 1

MAKE HIM KNOW YOU ARE IN LOVE

1. Make him believe that your love for him supersedes the one you have for any other. He will look special to you.

2. Let him practically see that your love is genuine and not conditional (not because of his wealth). You need to show him how you have soon missed him when you last met him by sending him love notes, giving him telephone calls at his work place or when he travels.

3. One very important key to make your man come for you more is the strong love you have for him. Men want to be told that they

are very handsome, hardworking, intelligent, good and very caring. Do this regularly with a genuine heart, he will come to believe in you since love develops when it is nurtured,Never say, “I love you”, to your partner without meaning it.

Module 2

RESPECT HIS PERSON AND OTHERS

4. The Oxford Advanced Learner's Dictionary defines respect as "polite behavior towards or care for somebody that you think is important and special to you, he deserves respect. No guy would want to come around a lady who doesn't respect his person.

5. Most ladies make so much mistakes by trying to always prove their point or by claiming to be right in everything. Don't sound pompous or as if you should take the final decision on issues. No man wants to share leadership with any woman. it is a man’s ego.

6. No man would love to marry any woman who ! doesn't respect people and whom people would not respect as well. if your man discovers that you don't have respect for your parents, his parents, friends, his brothers and sisters, no matter how much you try to treat him with respect, he will not be happy to continue with you in the relationship. So lady, treat people with respect and make yourself look respectable.

Module 3

BE FEMININE IN YOUR ATTITUDE

7. A woman should adore herself with good works and should possess a meek and quiet spirit. What will attract a man to a woman is her feminine qualities. if you are not feminine in your approach, and in the way you deal with other men around, your man will run away from you. No man wants to be pushed controlled or told what to do. Many ladies are domineering. While their men are passive in the relationship. A domineering woman makes her man less manly.

8. If a woman is too forward, the man might conclude that there is no way he can marry that type of girl, and that she cannot be the woman he is looking for in marriage, he will conclude that she is too strong for him, and too powerful for him. "If you say one, she will say ten'. This one does not need a man, she is a man herself. Ladies should be very

careful because, at.the point they have everything they need physically, financially and socially, their success could easily intimidate a man. But when a woman has all. of that but she is stilla woman of meek and gentile character, she will be loved by men.

9. As a woman, men can tolerate you and hang around you but will never marry you when you are not feminine in your attitude. Women should learn how to treat men. There are certain things that men look for in women. Even if he is not giving to marry you, he can recommend you. Men like respect, attention and honour. Let men feel like men around you a female. Do not argue or dominate. It is not going to work.

10. Every young lady would want the right person as a husband. You must make yourself a right person for you to attract a right person. So you must be flexible. The person you desire may have firm unyielding beliefs in a particular area, and your ability to go with the flow may help your relationship.

Always give you partner room to be himself without trying to change him to your mood.

Module 4

DON'T BE QURRELSOME /NAGGING

11. Don't be qurrelsome. Try always to be at peace with your guy through out your court ship period. No man loves to live with a nagging woman as a wife. Avoid a nagging habit to avoid disappointment. Learn to control your emotions or temperament. When you one thing with him and he has not answered you favorably and positively as you expected of him, don't rattle him, so as not to lead him to anger. Don't give your partner the

impression that this home will never be at peace.

12. The way you react to some issues or problems tell about your person tomorrow. When people in your office, home and church don't feel comfortable with yourbehaviour by the way you react irritably or by being quarrelsome in every little thing, you pose a threat to men when you do that. Men will be afraid of coming to you or to approach you for marriage. Anyone who wants todo that would be discouraged. Every man wants a peaceful home and no man wants a quarrelsome or nagging woman.

13. "It is better to dwell in a corner of the housetops, than with brawling woman in wide house". Prov. 21:9. If you are a woman having hot temper, you may be destroying your own relationship. You better cool your temper. If you get angry at every little thing even when your man begs you, you wouldn't listen until you do what is in your mind you will eventually loose your man.' So always be rational in your thought. Learn to tolerate your man's choice, decision and argument.

Module 5

DO NOT BE PROUD

14. Some ladies with high education, affluence, money etc., Display their bigness to the man that is around them. This scares a man away fyom you. Don't give your man an impression that you are too big. No decent man would love to marry a proud woman. Don't make your guy feel inferior before you.

15. Many ladies overprice themselves. When a woman sounds so costly by Insinuating that she is expensive and up there, she would only succeed in scaring men from her. Lady's actions and utterances suggests difficult conditions and unreachable demands as a price for her hand in marriage, she would indiréctly be telling, the man that, "shoes have sizes' and that she is not the man's

match. Many ladies have by so doing missed their God given Mr. Right.

Module 6

HUMBLE YOURSELF

16. When you are too pushy, when you are forward, when you are too aggressive, no man will want to come around you. No man likes a woman who knows it all. When you give men the impression that you know it all, they are going to feel that you don't need anybody in your life and they are going to move away from you.

17. If a man sees you are generally disrespectful lacking honor and you talk to people around you anyhow, a man will imagine the way you are going to treat him at home. What is important to me most is how men feel around you a woman. Does he feel he is less than a

man? Does he feel he is a slave? Does he feel weak he is around you that he does not know anything? Men do not want to be passive in any relationship, so they may disappoint you, and quit the relationship.

18. God made the man with ego. A man at the end of the day will end up being the husband and the head of the relationship. Every man has his ego. If you as a woman do not know how to handle the ego of a man; if you don't know how to nurse that ego; if you don't Know how to let him lead; if you don't know how to encourage him;if you don’t know how to complementhim; give him attention and take care of him; atthe end of the day, the man will feel that you are competing with him. So learn to move back and let your man lead or you will loose him.

Module 7

LEARN TO FORGIVE HIM

19. A man, G. K. Chesterton once said, "Forgiveness means, pardoning that which is unpardonable or it is no virtue at all." Forgiveness is a product of true love. Always pardon and over look your man's offences, accommodate his shortcomings, don't sound critical' and impatient with his fault and don't tell Him, "you, won't take nonsense in this relationship, you may loose him.

20. This does not mean you cannot correct him, but it should be in love, respect and be in submission, not criticizing him for almost everything. Men don't like to be criticized. When your man has offended you and apologises, forgive him and forget the offence.

21. One very important key to marriage success Is tolerance. You should be able to tolerate

your man and understand him. Be able to forgive and do not remind him of his faults in subsequent offences. The more you criticize and condemn him, the more likely you are going to drive your man away from you.

Module 8

HONOR HIM, HIS FRIENDS AND HIS PEOPLE.

22. Women need to honour their men because It makes them feel good. They needs to take good care of them. Don't sound like his mother reproving him for some childhood failure. No man likes to be made to feel like a small boy. Love and faith can win when petulant, demands fail. He will then learn to appreciate you as well.

23. Do you believe in your man? Do you consider him enough to worship? Do you regard and accept his person for who he is? Show him submission at all times and let him see that you would have a thing done this way but because you honour him you will let him have his way. With time, he will coine to work with your decision.

24. Your man will be very proud of you if his friends and relatives are speaking well of you. Never bring him down before his friends and people. Instead , honour him. Never quarrel, insult or keep malice with his people. Never ever criticize them no matter how bad you feel about them. Your husband to be may offer criticism of his parents, brothers and sister but to be,on the safe side, never join him. Even though he may feel hostile toward any of his friends or relatives or express resentment of his parents; he will never appreciate yout criticism.

Module 9

APPRECIATE AND PRAISE HIM ALWAYS.

25. Men generally need to be reminded of the good they havé done this will make them do more. There is a native parable that when you tell somebody thank you, you are asking the person to do more. Don't sound ungrateful; always express your gratitude to him for his kindness and love toward you. Appreciate his gift no matter how small they maybe.

26. Women need to praise their men, especially when you see him looking good. Always tell him how handsome, intelligent and nice he is and never compare him with another man. Stop talking about your old relationship. You make your man feel he is not the best for you.

27. Women should be proud of their men, so that when you go out together, you should be able to introduce him and say: "yeah, this is my husband to be." But if yo don't appreciate and respect him, there's no way you can be proud of him outside.

28. If you've gotten what you want from you man, continue to stroke his ego. With all the ills in the world, experts say he wants nothing more than for you to tell him what a wonderful mate he is. So sing his praises, and never let a day go by without expressing how pleased you are with him.

Module 10

LEARN TO ALWAYS PLEASE HIM.

29. Your man is a unique individual, different from every other persoh. As a woman, you have a strong desire, to please him, to keep

him happy and satisfied. You have to discover his special needs and work towards meeting them.

30. Discover your partner's sources of happiness and motivation and seek how you may please him. Let your man know that his joy is your strength and indeed to live for him is your highest earthly: happiness. Care for him, respect his feelings and wishes, reverence him and understand what makes him happy and what makes him angry.

Module 11

BE CONFIDENTIAL

31. Once your man has shared something secret with you in confidence, the very last thing you - should do is throw his secret back in his face. He may never open up to you again.

32. Always cover up his negative side. Never make public complain of your man a habit, which might make him to abandon you.

Module 12

DON'T BE TOO DEMANDING.

33. Many women make themselves too expensive to maintain. When you are too demanding you scare your man off. He may see you as an over taxing person and that you have come to just grab. It is better to lead a man to a point where he would shower you with gifts.

34. Avoid basty demands from your man. Men like women who are hard working and less demanding. if you over tax a man from the early days of courtship, it would mean that

you just came to grab from him and that could make him turn away from you.

35. Over demanding is a problem every lady should guide against. It makes the man to believe or see you as an individual not well brought up by your parents. And also, it can give him the impression that you will be a problem and a liability to him, so he may eventually leave you. Know it that, all your needs cannot be totally met. So to expect too much, you are inviting disaster.

36. Also, avoid demanding from every man that you see especially when your man is around. This will make him feel you are too cheap and that may allow these men have sec with you to reciprocate their kindness.

Module 13

GIVE HIM GIFTS ALSO

37. Men hold women in high esteem, who Surprise them with gifts; especially on his birthday, valentine's day, Christmas, New year, etc

38. Most women are so selfish that they believe that it is men who should spend for ladies always. When a man discovers that you always want to receive and grab from him, he would become mindful of this one thing that even after marriage you will not be willing to support him.

39. Try your best to support and assist him if he demands something of you. Don't be stingy with him. Men want women who are and and can assist them financially when they are married. So if you can afford it, buy him a suit, shoes, cream, wrist watch, handkerchief or books although these should be donc with wisdom so as not to appear as if you are bribing his love.

Module 14

YOU MUST BE FRUGAL/ ECONOMICAL

40. Any woman who is always discussing costly wedding with her man because she has developed a high taste will be scaring her man away, if the man feels he cannot meet up with a costly wedding. Women should learn to cut down on expenses.

41. A woman who wants to finish everything today and let tomorrow fend for itself will be discouraging her man. Spending ,money with high sense of responsibility and discipline, learn to spend your money well and not the other away round.

42. Every man will be please with a woman who will want hirh to save than spend it all. Give

him suggestion that will develop an investment mentality.

Module 15

CREATE TRUST AROUND YOUR PERSON.

43. Trust is a vital pillar for any marriage, relationship and any relationship without trust is dead already. A woman should be honest and sincere about financial issues, avoid deception, hypocrisy and lies.

44. Trust is a very important ingredient that is lacking in many courtships today. So do not give room for unnecessary suspicion from your man. Be transparent in your dealings

with him. Don't make yourself in trust able either by what you wear or the friends you keep.

45. Avoid unwholesome relationships with other men. Unhealthy familiarity and questionable closeness with the opposite sex could sends wrong signal to your man. This kill trust and breeds suspicion which in turn mar relationship.

Module 16

DON'T PRETEND, BE HONEST

46. A woman who is double dating will meet with disappointment. Many sisters because of the fear of disappointment, will choose to date two men at the same time; thereby

playing with their opportunity. If both men find out: they will desert you.

47. "An honest answer is like a kiss on the lip, Prov.24:26." No man will want to marry a dishonest woman. The day he discovers you are not honest; you tell lies; you are not truthful; you steal and cheat; you lose your man. Always tell him the truth and never lie.

48. Men don't like women who pretend. Try to be yourself. If you are wrong in the things you do, he can begin to correct you. Only be flexible, do not pretend. Disclose all the facts you know about yourself. Be very open. There are some women who hide the child or children that they had for somebody else in an earlier relationship, only for the man to discover the secret from others. This is unfair.

Module 17

BE VERY NEAT

49. You must keep Personal hygiene if you want your man to always come for you. Your hair must always be clean and look good. Fight against bad breath (mouth odour) by using mouth spray or mint sweets. Let your armpit always be shaved. Eradicate armpit odour by using antiperspirant or deodorants.

50. No man will be proud of a woman in public that have rashes, eczema or pimples. Take good care of your skin, use soap and cream that are good for your skin. Eradicate other private Odour on your body and keep your nails clean always.

51. Keep your home surroundings neat and tidy especially your room. A man went to visit his fiancee but was greeted with an unkept room pants and used clothes littering the bed and floor That was how he walked out of that relationship because he believed the girl was the lazy type and would not like to settle with such a person.

Module 18

YOUR APPERANCE.

52. Your personal apperance is very important you should "always endeavour to appear neat, clean and responsible. Make sure you are in the right colour and not like a rainbow due to multiple colour combination. Combined for every occasion. Dress to your frame because what look good on other people may not be good on you.

53. One of the first things that attracts a man to a woman is her looks or the way she dresses. The way a lady dresses tells what the lady is. It portrays your dignity. Some girls dress like old women in the name of religion or dress like a harlot. Dress like a young, godly and responsible lady he will respect you. For every man wants his wife to be an angel.

54. Dressing depicts character. A careless person, dress shabbily and a dirty person, puts on dirty and unkept clothes. Your physical appearance is the major point of attraction, and thus, must be neatly and beautifully packaged and presented if, public. The way you walk i.e your steps and carriage must be orderly and not awkward. The way you carry your bag as well, as all your public behaviour must be taken seriously.

55. Always avoid clothes that are suggestively tight, which show your features distinctly or clothes that reveal your nakedness and make you uncomfortable or make you like a harlot before your man. Some of these clothes girls put on, in the name of fashion totally mount up to madness. A responsible man will be put off. He will see you as a loose person.

56. There is way you dress that can easily make men scared of you. If you are opulent in your appearance always, men will begin to ask themselves if they can meet up with your high taste. The truth remains that sophisticated appearance is not best for a

woman who trusting God for marriage; for only few men would be courageous enough to marry women who are very rich, or heavily attired and represented always.

57. It is very important for you to be careful about what you allow into your system i.e your diet. Most ladies have problem with overweight. Avoid overeating. Cut down on fatty foods, and adjust your daily diet and food intake. Avoid much mineral and sugary food. They will make you grow out of shape.

58. Exercise is very important for every young lady. Don't be lazy. Exercise your body to keep it fit and together and avoid fatness and shapelessness.

Module 19

BE DILIGENT

59. In Genesis 2 God call woman an 'helpmate', that is to mean, a woman should assist, or support her man. So évery woman should have something doing, and have something to offer because no man wants to marry a liability or a parasite.

60. "She Seeketh wool and flax and worketh willingly with her hands; she is like the merchant's ship. She bringeth food from afar... "(Prov. 31 :13). A woman in court ship should show to her man that she will compliment his effort in the home after marriage by hard working in her job or business. Let diligence characterise your work. Every man would be encouraged by a woman who manages her business well and who does not waste money.

61. If you don't have what to do now, take up a job or create a job for yourself no matter how little it is. If you don't have education, take up a trade or learn a handwork. No man will want to settle for an idle woman. If you are in school or learning a trade, let your man see how diligent you are with what you are

doing. Read your books, do your assignment and pass your exam very well, he will be pleased with you.

Module 20

INSPIRE HIM TO GREATNESS.

62. Every man wants to marry a woman who would plan for the future with him, not the one, who wants to eat everything. This will strengthen the love he has for you. No man wants to marry a lady without knowing what she thinks, her principles and her future plans in life and to see whether he will be able to cope with her.

63. If you are able to inspire your man to do things in God's way, then at the end of the

day, that man will treat you with respect. He will honor you.

64. In courtship, inspire your man to do godly things God's way. You are not out to tempt him, so you have to watch the way you talk, walk, and the way you dress. Dress in an attractive way which is different from dressing to attract a man negativily.

65. Inside the marriage institution, the man is there to lead while the woman is there to inspire the man. Inspiring the man is different from telling him what to do. No! You are there to inspire in a gentle and meek way.

Module 21

BE A GOOD ADVISER.

66. Every man will be happy with a lady who will advise him to develop an investment mentality, and not one who is a waster.

67. You will win the heart of a man when he knows you are there to assist him in making right decisions. That is why you must cultivate endurance, be accommodating and patient to listen to him so that you can attend to every situation wisely.

68. Never advise or encourage your man to do evil but rather inspire your spouse to do things in God's way. At the end of the day, the man that you want to marry will try to behave like Christ to you.

Module 22

BE A GOOD COOK.

69. It is sad to know that many ladies do not know how to cook even with their education. "The way to man's heart, they say is the -

stomach”. It is a means to a man heart. Men want women who can cook them delicious meals.

70. | hear some girls say: ‘never mind, | will employ maids that will do the cooking for us. They have forgotten how many maids have taken husbands from many women because of their good foe and the manner with which they serve their meals. A man always like to appreciate a woman who has given him good food, and you may not be there to receive the praise. It is a dangerous signal, so learn to cook now.

71. ‘Failure in the kitchen’. in the name of civilization by ladies of marriageable age can be very embarrassing. Every lady must endeavour to prepare herself in this area. Remember, your man will be proud of you when his friends and relations commend you as a good cook.

Module 23

THE RIGHT USE OF TOUNGE.

72. Some ladies have discouraged their men from not marrying them because of the way they use their tongue. They don't have self control even in the presence of the man or the man's friends and relations, They behave anyhow and talk anyhow without shame and without minding who is watching them.

73. Try always to control your emotions. Don't be unnecessarily angry. Always be rational in your argument. Don't be harsh on your man, or even on other people. It is natural to argue over some matters or issues, but don't let your argument cause a fight or a quarrel. Learn to tolerate and use your tongue rightly. Don't try to win every argument.

74. A complaining tongue reveals an ungrateful heart. A refrained, bridled tongue breeds life and peace. Some women don't see any thing other than fault. Be careful how you use your tongue even if you must register any negative observation about your man, let it be done in love and say what you want to say at the right time with respect.

75. Be polite and not abusive to people whether he is your partner or not. Some ladies talk too much and rudely too. They will even want to rain thunder and brimstone ori any man who had approached them for marriage and whose educational status and financial ability had. been sized up as a mismatch. Don't forget that eyes are watching and that the victims of your tongue lash may discredit you, before your man and your relationship car be ruined.

Module 24

DON'T BE A TALKATIVE

76. In today’s world, one has to be very careful unfortunately, many women who are loose with their tongues discuss their secret with unfriendly friends thereby killing their marriage dreams.

77. Don't be a talkative or else you may not know when you will discuss your marriage plans with an Unfriendly person who may betray and ruin your courtship. Some ladies loose their men to friends.

78. Be careful how you tell your friends and your man’s relatives how he lavishes resources on you. So many Jealous eyes will be on you and will want to work on the relationship. Be careful.

79. Have some reservations even in being open to your guy. Some girls talk too much. All that happened in their home ten years ago will be narrated to the man. Everything that he told you in confidence will be’ heard by

your. man, from his parents or friends. This gives him the - impression that you can't be a good wife.

Module 25

BE PRAYERFUL

80. Spend time together frequently to pray and study the Bible together in order to lay a solid foundation for the union.

81. A woman who is very prayerful can avert disappointment from a man that is really from God for you. Being prayerful will also make God to see her through your courtship period.

82. To have a successful courtship and martiage tomorrow, you need to pray for patience Your man will definitely have faults which with patience, you can learn to live with. In (1 Cor.13) "Love is patient and kind". A mature love has this quality of patience , while an immature love wants immediate results. Give

up the tendency to complain, criticise and control, Knowing that you cannot control another human being.

83. You go a long way to win the heart of your man when he knows that you are there praying for him and hig business St Teresa once said ‘prayer is the morter that holds our house together’.

Module 26

HAVE FAITH IN HIS PERSON

84. Don't have fear of disappointment. In Jop 3:35, says “what I feared has come upon me”, Never you tell your man not to disappoint you or if he does not marry you, you will die! If you fear disappointment in your relationship, you will be disappointment.

85. Always tell your man that you trust him, because he is not like other men who disappoint girls. This will make him stand faithfully.

86. Every man is happy when you encourage his ego. Let him know that you believe in him, his capability in solving problems and in taking care of his responsibilities he will love more and be motivated to do more.

Module 27

IMPROVE ON YOUR SELF WORTH

87. Every man wit want to marry a woman that is well educated or that is well trained in any profession. So develop yourself further 'in

education or your trade. Be dynamic in your skills. The brighter your future, the more advantageous you are to your man. Don't remain where he met you. You can improve your education or training by running a part time programme.

88. Some ladies are hardly happy no matter what you do for them. They always put on moody Faces. Nobory can tell when they are happy or not. Such ladies scare away men from them. Try to work on your countenance and learn to forgive anyone who has offended you. Have a high self esteem or you loose your man.

89. Self confidence is one of the keys to a successful courtship and the key to it is believing in yourself. Always build a healthy self image. Think good about yourself, see yourself as unique and very important. Don't let your partner or any person look down on you. Uphold your self-esteem.

Module 28

BE MATURE

90. It is very amazing to observe that some grown up ladies still live with childish altitudes. They don't know their left from right. Some can't even Cook, and can't keep their houses clean. Some even cry for almost everything and do not know how to seceive and give back love. No man will accommodate such a woman. You must be mature enough to be adaptable, flexible and be sensitive to the needs of others regardless of your own feelings and needs.

Module 29

BE SOCIABLE AND HOSPITABLE.

91. Learn to be sociable. Be relevant and up date your dressing. Nobody wants to marry his grand mother ;so be modest and elegant. Look attractive - portray decorum.

92. Learn to use the cutlery, telephone and computer. Learn how to speak good English, work with your dictionary because it is embarrassing how some ladies today speak English.

93. Be hospitable, accommodating and friendly. Avoid rudeness, harshness, arrogance, etc. Sound sweet with people around you because your attitude with people around you because your attitude will determine how you will keep your man and sustain his love for you.

Module 30

AVOID PREMARITAL SEX.

94. For a woman to attract a man into a relationship she must convince the man that she is his friend. Keeping at the back of your mind that love is not SEX, neither is SEX love. Mature men do not look for SEX at the beginning of a relationship, but want his potential wife to show him friendship and love.

95. In many instances, sexual love making has been known to have overtaken partners before the end of courtship. This has led young people into wrong marriages that have no love in them. Sex blinds you to the reality of the relationship. The problem of giving sex as a show of love is that there are several other things that you must look for in a relationship that could be discovered in that person; rather, you see those things that look

like love, whereas , the love feeling is only a deception.

96. The over whelming attraction of physical beauty and material wealth, which causes the emotional feelings of lust and infatuation may actually look like love to you, but we all know they are not. Having sex with a man who commands the influences of lust and infatuation is not a show of love, but the commercialization: of sex. It shows you are ignorant of what you are looking for in a partner. You must agree with me that sex does not prove love: it is love that proves sex.

97. The threat that men impose on their women that if the woman love them, the woman must have sex with them is very wrong because, it is a condition whereby people try to use sex to prove love instead of allowing their love for 'each other to guide them into the ultimate consummation of their love. It is also wrong because sex is the last thing in a relationship of true love. Sexual love making is the consummation of love signaling the

commencement of marriage proper, not the prove of love at the beginning of courtship.

98. Rushing into sex with a man makes you cheap. And most ladies think that having sex with a man will make them get married quickly. This is no always the case ; instead it may cause a man to feel that the lady is loose and that there was nothing to look forward to anymore.

99. Don't rush into sex, no matter tl.a pressure from your man. Make him understand that you love tim and you expect him to wait till after the marriage ceremony. If he cannot wait but threatens to leave you, let him leave, he does not really love you. But if he loves you, he will wait and your love for each other will grow stronger and tomorrow he will trust you.

Module 31

HAVE EFFECTIVE COMMUNICATION

100. The best way to get to know your man is to listen to him, when you have a conversation. Don't judge him for what he has to say and don't interrupt him. If you want him to make more time for you, you have to make yourself available to listen. Lastiy, learn how and when to talk to your man about certain issues. Men love women who have wisdom and respect their time and Opinions. Also, give him your attention when he wants to talk to you; don't be carried away by friends and by some unnecessary things he will feel you don't have regard for him. So be careful. Lastly, call sometimes and tell him that he has a fine voice and you will want to

listen to him talk or sing to you. He will be very glad. Make sure all your time with him should be full of FUN, HE WILL KEEP ON COMING FOR YOU.

Story 1

Finally in Love!!

My name is Sarah Casey, but most of my friends prefer to call me Casey.. I guess it is because it is much easier to pronounce than "Sarah"

I'm the first child of my single mother, elder to my brother Peter.. At 16 years old, most of my feminine features were already out and clear like my curved hips, my oval face, my grown breasts and my shouting butts and this always needless to say attracted boys to me. I was in my year five in school and most days when I'm coming back from school I always have various boys trying to get my attention and unfortunately to them I wasn't giving it, the last thing I want to do is to be seen as a whore or as the cheap type.

The boys are saying that I'm rude, yea it was my self defense mechanism, little did I know it was going to end sooner or later and I'm the one who is going to do away with it.

My Mother.

My mother is a single mother I never happened to see my father, when I was fourteen years old I ask my mom about my dad and she told me that when she was in the last year of her high school she fell in love with a guy, who she called Terence and according to the description she gave as much as I can remember she said he is about 180 cm in height and he was a blond with sort of blue eyes, the way my mother blushes when talking about him suggest that no doubt he is an extremely handsome man.

My mother said the lived together in a small house they rented after her highschool, away from her father, there they gave birth to me and about a year later my brother came, they wanting to relocate to a new and quiet environment decided to move over to xx, while still on the prospect of moving over to a new environment my father suddenly disappeared with most of my mother's money, then my mom was the bread winner because she was a certified registered nurse and earning a very substantial amount, my mother did everything she can to locate him but she couldn't and she wept long enough for him, not for the money but for the love she had for him. I didn't fathom what type of love is this little did I know I will soon find myself in such a situation.

Back to my school I was loved or will I rather say lust over by many boys but strangely enough I wasn't just interested, so I didn't give a hoot about their advances.

One day I came to school only to hear rumors about me being a lesbian, fine, I wasn't an introvert and I was sort of so close to girls and I didn't give a much of a hoot to the opposite sex, maybe because I feel as that they were just after my body, you know. But you have to trust me I was no lesbian.

There was a boy who was my classmate and I do see him along my street, and he was so handsome, I have to admit and unlike most of the other boys in my class who tries to get my attention. Naturally I was attracted to him, I couldn't just help it.

One day after school hours I stayed back in school to do some assignment, because I know my mom won't be back by now, she went to her father's house to visit her ailing mother, as I was through with my assignment the weather got so bad that I needed no soothsayer to tell me that it would rain. As I was gathering my books quickly so as to try my hardest in beating the heavy cloud I heard same shuffling of books and almost ran into the boy from my street I later learnt his name is Mike, we greeted out selves warmly as though we have been "friends "......

www.ingramcontent.com/pod-product-compliance
Lightning Source LLC
LaVergne TN
LVHW050345160826
845677LV00014B/3795

9798361480593